Which Toy Do You Want?

Seed
Learning

Which toy do you want?

I want this motorcycle.

I want this silver
motorcycle.

Which toy
do you want?

I want this race car.

I want this gold
race car.

Which toy
do you want?

I want this
ambulance.

I want this white
ambulance.

Which toy
do you want?

I want this
garbage truck.

I want this green garbage truck.

Which toy
do you want?

I want this
fire truck.

I want this red
fire truck.

Which toy
do you want?

I want this
helicopter.

I want this black helicopter.

Which toy do you want?

I want this bicycle.

I want this orange
bicycle.

Let's learn about Mid-Autumn Festival.

October

Sunday	Monday	Tuesday	Wednesday	Thursday	Friday	Saturday
				(1)	2	3
4	5	6	7	8	9	10
11	12	13	14	15	16	17
18	19	20	21	22	23	24
25	26	27	28	29	30	31

Trace the word October and circle the date.